Birds Of San Pedro Martir, Lower California

A. W. Anthony

In the interest of creating a more extensive selection of rare historical book reprints, we have chosen to reproduce this title even though it may possibly have occasional imperfections such as missing and blurred pages, missing text, poor pictures, markings, dark backgrounds and other reproduction issues beyond our control. Because this work is culturally important, we have made it available as a part of our commitment to protecting, preserving and promoting the world's literature. Thank you for your understanding.

BIRDS

— OF —

SAN PEDRO MARTIR

LOWER CALIFORNIA

— BY —

A. W. ANTHONY

[Extract from Zoe, Vol. IV, No. 3, issued October 9, 1893]

BIRDS OF SAN PEDRO MARTIR, LOWER CALIFORNIA.

BY A. W. ANTHONY.

Mr. W. E. Bryant's excellent Catalogue of the Birds of Lower California has left but little to record from the northern part of that peninsula, but the notes furnished by the present writer were necessarily very fragmentary owing to the collections as well as many notes being inaccessible at the time. It is to correct this deficiency and at the same time record the observations of a trip through that region the past season that the present paper is offered. The expedition crossed the national boundary at Tia Juana, fifteen miles from San Diego, on April 17, 1893, and proceeded by easy stages to the western base of San Pedro Martir by way of Ensenada and Colnett. The first benches of the mountain were not reached until May 5.

Several days were spent at various camps between this point (7000 feet) and the gulf slope which was not reached until May 23. The return march was taken up May 27 and San Diego reached June 7.

During our southward march the migration was at its height and at the time that we left the higher parts of the mountain new arrivals were seen almost daily; it is not improbable that among these late arrivals some Sonoran species might have been found had our time permitted a more thorough investigation. It is probable, however, that most of the species inhabiting the pine belt were noted. The region embraced in the name of San Pedro Martir consists of a high plateau of about sixty-five or seventy miles in length by twenty in width, lying about twenty miles from the gulf, and with its greatest extent parallel with that coast. Most of the plateau would be embraced within the limits of 30° and 31° north latitude. The northern end rises to a height, in one or two peaks, of 12,500 feet, estimated, and from that point the ridges and peaks drop away by degrees until at the southern end they merge into the low, barren hills, common to the peninsula at this point. The east and northern slopes, however, are very steep and rocky, with only two or three almost impassable trails, while the eastern side presents along its entire length in many places a sheer precipice for thousands of feet.

A series of large open meadows is found at an elevation of 8000 to 8500 feet, surrounded by rough, rocky ridges and heavy pine timber. These ridges are characteristic of the entire region which is composed of soft, friable syenite, the softer parts of which in crumbling away have left huge masses of gigantic boulders forming ridges, in many cases impassable. A growth of yellow pine, *Pinus Jeffreyi*, covers the ridges and slopes as low as 7000 feet altitude, where it gives place to a belt of scattered piñons, *P. Parryana*, reaching to 6000 feet or less, a growth of Manzanita and Ceanothus covers all of the slopes and ridges where it is too rocky for the pines to obtain a foot-hold, and in many places a small shrub oak was abundant. The streams, which were abundant, were all fringed with willow and a few Aspens were seen in some localities. Arising as this region does from a sea of barren dry hills and reaching an elevation higher than any point south of Mt. Whitney, California, it is not strange that its fauna should be unusually interesting although its relationship is with that of the northern mountains.

The birds observed in the pine belt were limited as to species, but abundant individually. A few species were limited to certain localities and were not plenty, but as a rule all were generally distributed. The list has been somewhat extended to embrace a few species not belonging to the mountain region, but unless otherwise stated, all species were found on or about the mountain.

The following species are for the first time recorded from the peninsula:

Carpodacus cassini.

Peucæa ruficeps.

Melospiza fasciata heermanni.

Passerella iliaca megarhyncha.

Troglodytes aëdon aztecus.

Phalacrocorax penicillatus. BRANDT'S CORMORANT. In April, 1889, I was told of a cormorant that had been about my camp at Valladares, six miles from the base of San Pedro. A short time afterwards I found its body in the creek. It had evidently strayed from the coast and followed up the stream until, unable to find its way back, it had starved. A single bird of this species, or *albociliatus*, was seen at San Telmo, ten miles from the coast, April 30.

Anas boschas. MALLARD. Quite a number were nesting in the large meadows on top of the mountain when we arrived, May 13. A nest of eggs, on the point of hatching, was found by my brother, W. W. Anthony, May 17; the nest was placed in a hole under a pile of boulders by the side of the stream and very well hidden.

Anas cyanoptera. CINNAMON TEAL. A few pairs were nesting in La Grulla meadows, May 13. In October, 1887, this meadow was visited and large flocks of ducks of several species were found in shallow ponds formed by the early rains. They cannot, of course, winter in this region, as it is subject to a fall of not less than six feet of snow, according to native testimony. Mr. Bryant has quoted me as reporting *A. carolinensis* at 9000 feet in winter, a mistake due to my own carelessness, probably. The species was found at that altitude in fall, but not above 1500 feet after November.

Plegadis guarauna. WHITE-FACED GLOSSY IBIS. At San Telmo they were usually seen during summer in small numbers about a large marsh above the settlement, and I think they doubtless bred there. Adults and young were shot at San Quintin in October.

Tantalus loculator. WOOD IBIS. In the fall a few wood ibis are to be found in all of the marshes and streams from Ensenada to Santa Maria.

Botaurus lentiginosus. AMERICAN BITTERN. Common in the marshes at Colnett and San Ramon, where it doubtless nests.

Ardea herodias. GREAT BLUE HERON. Common at San Quintin and north of that point, also seen to some extent inland. A colony was found nesting on San Martin Island on April 12. At this date most of the nests contained young, but one set of three fresh eggs were taken.

Ardea candidissima. SNOWY HERON. Very common all along the coast from El Rosario north. I think they nest at San Ramon, as they were seen at that point all summer.

Ardea rufa. REDDISH EGRET. Not uncommon at San Quintin.

Fulica americana. AMERICAN COOT. Coots were seen occasionally along the creek below Valladares in the fall. Young were found at San Telmo as early as April 1. A pair was found nesting on San Pedro in May, 1889.

Recurvirostra americana. AMERICAN AVOCET. Not uncommon at San Quintin, Colnett and Ensenada in fall, only seen, however, about the fresh water marshes.

Actitis macularia. SPOTTED SANDPIPER. One was seen at La Grulla, on San Pedro, May 14. Rather common along the coast.

Ægialites vocifera. KILLDEER. A few were found in all the meadows on top of the mountain.

Oreortyx pictus confinis. SAN PEDRO PARTRIDGE. Since describing this race, I have secured a series of skins from San Diego County, California, that are practically identical with my skins from Lower California, San Pedro and Valladares, thus making it necessary to either ignore the Lower California bird, or to include Southern California in its habitat. I am unable to secure specimens from the type locality at present, and so cannot determine the status of the race beyond a doubt.

A single skin from the collection of the California Academy of Sciences, from Monterey, is slightly darker above and shows a conspicuous rusty edging to several of the secondaries, forming a patch on the closed wing not seen in any of my southern birds.

During the past season partridges were found in abundance all over San Pedro Martir and fresh eggs were taken from the time of our arrival May 5 to the last day, May 28.

In the Gaudaloupe Valley, forty miles south of Ensenada, several Oreortyx were seen in the thick chaparral of Ceanothus, almost down to the coast.

Callipepla californica vallicola. VALLEY PARTRIDGE. In October, 1887, this species was found to be quite common on San Pedro as high as La Grulla 8200 feet. It was again met with in April and May 1889 and the past season, but in comparatively small numbers. Birds taken in May (5th to 25th) contained in several cases eggs ready to be deposited.

Capt. C. E. Bendire, in "Life Histories of North American Birds," has recorded my observations regarding the non-nesting of this species during very dry seasons; this habit was again noticed the past season and under very favorable conditions.

Upon our return trip from the base of the mountain to San Diego the present species was abundant, but it was only in the well-watered valleys that they were paired or that young were seen. The past winter and spring had been unusually dry and in many valleys water was entirely absent and vegetation generally very scant and dry. In such localities quail were all in flocks and those that were shot showed little if any enlargement of the ovaries. Small young were seen at San Telmo, a well-watered valley, on May 30.

Pseudogryphus californianus. CALIFORNIA VULTURE. The first evidence that I found of the occurrence of the condor in Lower California was the finding of a dead bird in Guadaloupe Valley, forty miles south of Ensenada and near the coast; later another carcass was found in the dry barren hills east of El Rosario, about 30° north, which was the most southern point where positive evidence of its occurrence was obtained. My brother, W. W. Anthony, reported seeing these birds at one time near Real Del Castillo in the San Rafael Valley.

On San Pedro Martir they are of rather common occurrence, being seen daily about the meadows at altitudes of 8000 and 9000 feet. The Indians told me that their nests were to be found on the high cliffs of the gulf slope and others informed me that they built in the tops of large pines.

I greatly doubt the last statement, however. Every Indian and Mexican gold miner is provided with from one to six of the primary quills of this species for carrying gold dust, the open end being corked with a plug of soft wood and the primitive purse hung from the neck by a buckskin string. All of the dead birds that I saw in Lower California had been killed for their quills alone.

Cathartes aura. TURKEY VULTURE. Common during the summer all over the mountain, usually seen in company with the condor and raven.

Parabuteo unicinctus harrisi. HARRIS'S HAWK. Through some mistake my notes on this species were included under the head of *Buteo lineatus elegans* in Mr. Bryant's list. During the last season Harris' hawk was seen in one or two valleys between Ensenada and Colnett, and in one or two places on San Pedro as high as 7000 feet. It was nowhere common, however.

Buteo borealis calurus. WESTERN REDTAIL. Very common throughout the northern part of the peninsula, and found nesting in abundance in the pines on San Pedro. Nearly all of the pairs seen last spring consisted of one very light colored and one melanistic bird. At La Grulla a pair of redtails were nesting near our camp. The male was a very light bird, while the female was so dark as to be several times mistaken for the dark phase of *swainsoni*. On May 16 the female was shot as she rose from the nest, and on skinning her I found in her stomach the remains of a *Cyanocephalus* and a nearly complete rattlesnake that must have measured over two feet in length. On the following day the male was seen flying about the nest with another female fully as dark as his former mate, and I was surprised to see her feeding young ten days or two weeks old. I had supposed the nest still contained eggs. As it was such a clear case of adoption I concluded to leave them undisturbed, but the unfortunate male was doomed a few days later to lose his second mate which was shot by a member of our party; upon dissection this bird was also found to have a large rattlesnake coiled up in her stomach. We frequently saw redtails sailing about over the meadows with large snakes hanging from their talons.

Buteo elegans lineatus. RED-BELLIED HAWK. Not seen this season south of Ensenada. It seems to be confined chiefly to the creek bottoms where cottonwood and sycamore growths afford it convenient nesting sites.

My notes on this species in Mr. Bryant's list refer to Parabuteo.

Buteo abbreviatus. ZONE-TAILED HAWK. On April 24, 1889, two pairs were found nesting on San Pedro at elevations of 7000 and 7500 feet, and one of the birds secured. The past season only an occasional stray bird was seen, not over four or five, and no nests were observed.

Buteo swainsoni. SWAINSON'S HAWK. One of the most common species in all of the lower valleys, but does not seem to extend very high up on the mountain, as I do not remember seeing it above 3000 feet. One that I shot in the Guadaloupe Valley on April 24 had its inner secondaries and tail feathers so badly burned as to render it unfit for the cabinet. The only explanation seems to be that the bird was hunting near some of the brush fires in the valley and attempted to take a rabbit or other game too near the fire, or perhaps it was attempting to cook its dinner.

Aquila chrysaëtos. GOLDEN EAGLE. No eagles were seen

on San Pedro the past season; they appear to be very rare there. At San Telmo a pair have for years nested in a cliff about ten miles from the coast, where they were seen in April of the present year.

Falco sparverius sub. sp.(?) SPARROW HAWK. One or two sparrow hawks were seen on top of San Pedro, but as no specimens are in the collection I am unable to say which race occurs there.

Strix pratincola. AMERICAN BARN OWL. Very common in the lower valleys, but not observed above the live oak belt at 3500 feet.

Syrnium occidentale. SPOTTED OWL. An owl that I think was this species was flushed from a live oak on the slope of San Pedro at about 4500 feet elevation. Mr. Bryant has recorded a bird that I saw near the same place in 1887.

Megascops asio trichopsis.(?) MEXICAN SCREECH OWL. Screech owls have several times been seen and heard between the coast and the top of San Pedro, but as no specimens were secured the exact position of the sub-species is somewhat doubtful.

Bubo virginianus subarcticus. WESTERN HORNED OWL. Very common in the pine timber of San Pedro and in the coast valleys where there is timber enough to afford it shelter.

Speotyto cunicularia hypogæa. BURROWING OWL. Seen in several of the valleys between Tia Juana and San Telmo. I think none were seen above that point. On June 9 an entire family were seen in the Carriso Valley, perched on the bushes about the burrow.

Glaucidium sp. (?) PIGMY OWL. At Valladares, near the base of the mountain, two were seen by a member of our party, but not secured.

Geococcyx californianus. ROAD-RUNNER. Common in the lower valleys and slopes of the mountain. One was reported to me from 7000 feet.

Ceryle alcyon. BELTED KINGFISHER. One was heard on two or three occasions at La Grulla, on San Pedro. Common on the coast in winter.

Dryobates villosus hyloscopus. CABANIS'S WOODPECKER. Not uncommon in the pines on San Pedro. Given as *harrisii* in my notes in Mr. Bryant's list.

Dryobates scalaris lucasanus. ST. LUCAS WOODPECKER. A specimen taken April 30 at San Telmo and others seen. I have frequently seen *Dryobates* in the cacti along the coast hills from San Fernando north, but owing to their extreme shyness have usually failed to take specimens. It is quite probable that the notes furnished Mr. Bryant regarding the finding of *D. nuttallii* among the cacti of the coast belong to the present species, as I do not think I have ever seen *nuttallii* away from deciduous trees.

Dryobates nuttallii. NUTTALL'S WOODPECKER. Common along all the timbered streams as high as 4000 feet, or the limit of the live oaks and sycamores.

Melanerpes formicivorus bairdi. CALIFORNIA WOODPECKER. Well distributed through the pines on San Pedro, and probably resident; nowhere very plenty, but more common in the oak growth from Ensenada north.

Colaptes cafer. RED-SHAFTED FLICKER. Rather common on San Pedro, descending to the lower valleys in winter.

Phalænoptilus nuttallii californicus. CALIFORNIA POOR-WILL. Poor-wills were very abundant in the lower valleys in late April of the past year, but none were heard above 4500 feet until May 8, when one was heard at our camp at 7000 feet. They were heard at 8500 feet May 25, and one taken at the western edge of the mountain on May 28 was evidently nesting. They were much oftener heard than seen, as they are not much on the wing.

Chordeiles texensis. TEXAS NIGHT-HAWK. Quite common in the lower valleys, especially about the water holes; one seen as high as La Grulla—8200 feet.

Cypseloides niger. BLACK SWIFT. At San Telmo a pair of these swifts appeared about camp several times during the forenoon of April 30th, and one was shot by a member of the party; not noticed again.

Chætura vauxii. VAUX'S SWIFT. At Tia Juana April 16,

I found a small flock of these swifts flying about over a pool of water in company with *Petrochelidon* and *Tachycineta thalassina*. Later they were seen in several localities as far south as Colnett and San Telmo; at this point they were quite common April 30, and evidently migrating in company with swallows. A single bird was seen at La Grulla May 18.

Aëronautes melanoleucus. WHITE-THROATED SWIFT. Seen in several valleys between Tia Juana and the base of San Pedro but all evidently migrating. On top of the mountain they appeared about our camp by dozens and could easily have been taken in large numbers; they were mating and preparing to nest in the high cliffs on the eastern side of the mountain where I found them in 1889. A small colony was found nesting in the cliffs at San Ysidro in May, 1887. On the Coronado Islands, twenty miles from San Diego, a colony was discovered nesting in a cliff overhanging the surf, not over thirty feet above the water, but as usual the nests were inaccessible.

Calypte costae. COSTA'S HUMMINGBIRD. Very abundant in all of the valleys along the coast and base of the mountain; not seen in the pines until about May 20; on May 28 they were building at 7500 feet.

Calypte annae. ANNA'S HUMMINGBIRD. A very common resident of the coast region; not seen until May 15 at La Grulla. As this species, as well as the preceding, nest in March, sometimes as early as February in the lower valleys, it is not at all improbable that the birds that we found in May on the mountain had raised a brood before migrating.

Tyrannus verticalis. ARKANSAS KINGBIRD. One was seen May 15 at La Grulla, the only one seen in the pines; very common in the coast valleys.

Myiarchus cinerascens. ASH-THROATED FLYCATCHER. A few were seen on San Pedro in 1889, and again the past season, but it was not at all abundant; in the lower valleys it is more common. A nest and set of four fresh eggs were taken from a hollow on an elder in the Guadaloupe Valley, June 2.

Sayornis saya. SAY'S PHŒBE. Quite common along the base of the mountain and in all of the coast valleys below 4000 feet. At Valladares they were given to nesting in all of the deserted mines, and I have found their nests twenty feet below the surface of the ground in an old shaft or tunnel.

Sayornis nigrescens. BLACK PHŒBE. Quite common along all of the water courses and resident as high as 3000 feet at least; a single pair were nesting at La Grulla May 22.

Contopus borealis. OLIVE-SIDED FLYCATCHER. Abundant throughout the pine belt, one in my collection from that region has a large, clear, white patch on the throat, lacking entirely the streaking common to that species.

Contopus richardsonii. WESTERN WOOD PEWEE. Very common in San Pedro; one that had its nest in a large pine over our camp on the night of May 28, kept up a calling at intervals of thirty minutes all night.

Empidonax cineritius. ST. LUCAS FLYCATCHER. Very common all over the mountain, especially along the streams and in the willows. It was evidently nesting at the time of my visit in May, but no eggs were taken. From its preference for willow thickets at this time I would expect to find its nests in such places as *E. wrightii* might choose.

Empidonax pusillus. LITTLE FLYCATCHER. Seen only during migrations.

Otocoris alpestris chrysolæma. MEXICAN HORNED LARK. Along the coast as far as Colnett, at least the horned lark belongs to this race as shown by specimens in my collection. At San Quintin, however, fifty miles further south, *pallida* is the race met with during the breeding season if not the entire year. Mr. Townsend's types of *pallida* came from the region just east of San Pedro, which with the San Quintin record on the west led me to expect this form from the mountain meadows. No larks were met with, however, until the eastern edge was reached; here a few were taken that were all true *chrysolæma*.

Otocoris alpestris pallida. SONORAN HORNED LARK. My notes were given to Mr. Bryant and published by him under the name of *rubea*. It seems, however, from the material I have at present that *pallida* is the form found at San Quintin during the nesting season, giving away to *chrysolæma* a short distance to the north and east.

Aphelocoma californica obscura. BELDING'S JAY. The status of this race is in a condition similar to that of the San Pedro Partridge as already stated. San Diego County birds are indistinguishable from those from San Pedro, but I am unable to secure typical *californica* from Monterey, the type locality. It seems, however, from the series now on hand as if *obscura* would have to be reduced to a synonym of *californica*.

Corvus corax sinuatus. AMERICAN RAVEN. Very common from the coast to the highest point visited on San Pedro.

Picicorvus columbianus. CLARK'S NUTCRACKER. In May, 1889, a single specimen was secured at La Grulla from a flock of *Cyanocephalus*. Later the fragments of another were found where they had been left by a hawk or owl; not met with in 1893.

Cyanocephalus cyanocephalus. PIÑON JAY. Very abundant in the pines on San Pedro. Those taken had their stomachs full of beetles and insects that they had caught in the grassy meadows.

Icterus cucullatus nelsoni. ARIZONA HOODED ORIOLE. Very common along the base of the mountain and in all of the lower valleys, but not seen above the live oaks at 4500 feet.

Scolecophagus carolinus. RUSTY BLACKBIRD. The capture of a single specimen at the base of the mountain has been recorded in Mr. Bryant's list.

Scolecophagus cyanocephalus. BREWER'S BLACKBIRD. Common in all of the lower valleys; at San Vincente a large colony had taken possession of the old olive trees at the abandoned mission and dozens of nests with eggs were seen on April 28. At La Grulla they were nesting in the pines in early May; they were not noticed away from the large meadows, however.

Carpodacus cassini. CASSIN'S PURPLE FINCH. Not uncommon on San Pedro in the pines where it is probably resident; often seen in flocks of the following but very shy and difficult to secure. Not given in Bryant's list.

Carpodacus mexicanus frontalis. HOUSE FINCH. Abundant resident in all of the lower valleys; on San Pedro a few only were found upon our arrival, May 5, but they soon became abundant, especially about the meadows. Specimens from that region are not materially different from Southern California skins in my collection.

Spinus tristis. AMERICAN GOLDFINCH. A few winter about the base of the mountain.

Spinus psaltria. ARKANSAS GOLDFINCH. A common resident about the northern part of the peninsula reaching the lower slope of the mountain.

Spinus lawrencei. LAWRENCE'S GOLDFINCH. Common with the preceding species; not seen above 4000 feet on San Pedro.

Spinus pinus. PINE SISKIN. Well distributed through the pines on San Pedro, but undoubtedly not common; no nests were found.

Ammodramus sandwichensis alaudinus. WESTERN SAVANNA SPARROW. A few winter about the base of San Pedro.

Ammodramus rostratus. LARGE BILLED SPARROW. Very common in fall and winter all along the coast, but never wandering far from salt water. It is considerable of a mystery to me to locate the nesting grounds of this species. Thousands of birds are seen in all of the salt marshes along the coast from the northernmost limit of its range. No decrease is noticed in their numbers until the nesting season approaches, when they suddenly disappear and are not again noticed until August, when they make their appearance with young, and are common about the old haunts until the following spring.

On one occasion Mr. A. M. Ingersoll discovered at San Diego a bird carrying food for its young, but was unable to find the nest owing to the great distance to which the bird flew with its load. On the beach in April, 1887, I shot a female at San Ramon that had undoubtedly left her eggs but a few moments before. As the birds were scarce at that point and I was unacquainted with the rarity of their eggs, I made no effort to find their nests, and, although I have patiently searched for them ever since, I have never again seen birds during the nesting season. The character of the ground at San Ramon, where a few were undoubtedly nesting, was a broad sand beach, covered with drift-wood, flanked by a few sand dunes, back of which was a series of small lagoons of brackish water, thickly grown to tules. The eggs of this species which are frequently offered to the public by local collectors of Southern California have, so far as my observations have gone, always been taken from the nests of *A. beldingi*.

Zonotrichia leucophrys. WHITE-CROWNED SPARROW.

Zonotrichia leucophrys intermedia. INTERMEDIATE SPARROW.

Zonotrichia leucophrys gambeli. GAMBEL'S SPARROW. All of the white crowns are abundant about the base of San Pedro during the winter months, and a few are to be seen in the pines during migrations. But few specimens were taken and the comparative abundance of the different species was not determined.

Zonotrichia coronata. GOLDEN-CROWNED SPARROW. Quite common during the migrations with the white crowns but seems to winter farther south than the bulk of these species. All of the *coronata* taken in April were moulting and unfit for specimens.

Spizella socialis arizonæ. WESTERN CHIPPING SPARROW. Very abundant about the base of the mountain and resident; one was shot at 7000 feet elevation May 10.

Spizella atrigularis. BLACK-CHINNED SPARROW. Rather common in the hills from the coast to the base of the mountain. I have no specimens from the pine belt, but am sure that its song was heard in May, 1887, at 10,000 feet elevation.

Junco hyemalis thurberi. THURBER'S JUNCO. It is quite probable that all of the Lower California records of *oregonus* belong to the present species. I found them about the base of San Pedro in winter with *townsendi*, and met with them in the Burro Cañon north of Ensenada April 23, the past season.

Junco townsendi. TOWNSEND'S JUNCO. Very abundant throughout the pine region of San Pedro, only reaching the lower elevations in winter. The past season the juncos were found building upon our arrival in the pines, May 5, but no eggs were found until the 10th. A set of three were taken at La Grulla on the 14th, that were about to hatch. The nest was in an old woodpecker's hole in a large pine that had been blown down, with its top resting on a big boulder. The hole which was about six feet from the ground was on the under side of the trunk and the nest about on a level with the opening; it was composed of dry grasses and lined with deer hair. A nest which was found on May 26 in a hole in a rotten stub about ten feet from the ground contained three eggs slightly incubated. A number of nests, which were found under logs, boulders and similar locations and left for full sets, were all destroyed. Several birds were shot while carrying large bills full of deer hair for nest lining.

Peucæa ruficeps. RUFOUS-CROWNED SPARROW. A series of four skins taken between Tia Juana and the base of San Pedro are practically indistinguishable from Southern California examples; seems to be rather common in a few favored localities along the base of San Pedro.

Melospiza fasciata heermanni. HEERMANN'S SONG SPARROW. Through an error I referred the San Pedro song sparrows to *rivularis* in my notes published by Mr. Bryant. They seem to be true *heermanni*, however. Along the creeks and about water holes this form is more or less abundant from San Diego to the top of San Pedro.

Passerella iliaca megarhyncha. THICK-BILLED SPARROW. A few were seen in October on San Pedro and on one or two subsequent occasions at Valladares.

Pipilo maculatus megalonyx. SPURRED TOWHEE. Not uncommon in the Manzanita and shrub oak growth on San Pedro.

Pipilo fuscus crissalis. CALIFORNIAN TOWHEE. Very abundant along the lower slopes of the mountain, but rather rare in the timbered regions; confined here chiefly to the rocky ridges and Manzanita growth.

Habia melanocephala. BLACK-HEADED GROSBEAK. Quite common during migrations along the base of the mountain; a few were seen as high as 4000 feet and were probably nesting at that altitude.

Guiraca cærulea eurhyncha. WESTERN BLUE GROSBEAK. Very common in all the coast valleys from San Quintin northward; usually seen in the region of cultivated fields and willow thickets. They were seen in the San Telmo up to within a short distance of the mountain.

Passerina amœna. LAZULI BUNTING. Abundant with the preceding species, with which it was often seen; one or two were seen on top of the mountain.

Piranga ludoviciana. LOUISIANA TANAGER. Quite common; not seen above 7000 feet.

Progne subis hesperia. WESTERN MARTIN. Very common; nesting in colonies from Valladares, 2500 feet altitude, throughout the pines.

Petrochelidon lunifrons. CLIFF SWALLOW. Common in colonies from the coast to the top of the mountain; they were found nesting on the sides of huge granite boulders in meadows of La Grulla May 13, and later on the eastern side.

Chelidon erythrogastra. BARN SWALLOW. A few were noted on top of the mountain; more common along the coast.

Tachycineta thalassina. VIOLET-GREEN SWALLOW. Very abundant from Valladares to the top of the mountain; nesting in hollow pines throughout the region visited. On May 19 a large number of females gathered about camp attracted by the feathers of some mallards that had been shot for the table. Usually the coveted feather was secured without the ceremony of alighting, the bird hovering over the pile until a feather was selected, and then securing it by a dainty dip of the head and immediately dashing off to the nest. A day or so later I shot a junco from a tall pine, which in falling detached a number of feathers. These were almost instantly secured by a flock of these swallows, and before a feather had reached the ground they were all appropriated with the exception of one long white rectrix which was several times caught and as often rejected.

Ampelis cedrorum. CEDAR WAXWING. Rather common about Valladares, where a specimen was secured May 4. I have never seen any on San Pedro, but several times thought that I heard their call notes.

Phainopepla nitens. PHAINOPEPLA. Very common at certain times about the base of the mountain up to about 6000 feet.

Vireo solitarius cassinii. CASSIN'S VIREO. Not uncommon in the pines where it was first seen May 13; it became more common a week or so later.

Vireo bellii pusillus. LEAST VIREO. Very common all along the base of the mountain, but probably not reaching above the live oaks at 4500 feet.

Helminthophila celata lutescens. LUTESCENT WARBLER. Seen along the western base of the mountain and in all the lower valleys during the spring migration.

Dendroica æstiva. YELLOW WARBLER. Common during migrations in the valleys and as a summer resident in the higher altitudes. A single skin in my collection from La Grulla, No. 4031, May 15, is the brightest colored specimen I have ever seen from any locality, and also differs from others in my series in having a well defined dark shaft streak along the inner web of the tail feathers, occupying half of the web which is yellow to the shaft in all *æstiva* that I have examined. Unfortunately the specimen is the only one I have from that region, and I am unable to say how constant the character may prove to be.

Dendroica auduboni. AUDUBON'S WARBLER. Very abundant during migrations; one taken at La Grulla, May 13.

Dendroica nigrescens. BLACK-THROATED GRAY WARBLER. Rather common as a summer resident in the pine belt, nesting in the Manzanita thickets.

Dendroica townsendi. TOWNSEND'S WARBLER. During the past spring this warbler was first met with in the Burro Cañon, where a dozen or more were seen in the live oaks, April 23. As they were quite restless and somewhat difficult to identify, it is not improbable that *occidentalis* also occurred at this same place. They were again met with at Valladares, May 3, and on the following day on the west side of San Pedro at each of these localities they were quite common in the live oaks with *D. nigrescens* and *occidentalis.*

Dendroica occidentalis. HERMIT WARBLER. Quite common at Valladares and on San Pedro at 4500 feet; several were taken at each camp.

Geothlypis trichas occidentalis. WESTERN YELLOW-THROAT. A female was taken at La Grulla, May 1, 1889; not uncommon about the base of the range.

Icteria virens longicauda. LONG-TAILED CHAT. Common in the lower valleys, but only seen occasionally along the base of the mountain.

Sylvania pusilla pileolata. PILEATED WARBLER. Before we left the pine belt, this warbler had become common along the streams; more abundant, however, in the lower valleys during migrations.

Anthus pensilvanicus. AMERICAN PIPIT. A few seen in May, 1889, on the eastern edge of the mountain; abundant along the coast in winter.

Mimus polyglottos. MOCKINGBIRD. Probably does not extend above 5000 feet on the western slope of the mountain.

Harporhynchus redivivus. CALIFORNIA THRASHER. Not uncommon in the Manzanitas at 7000 feet, but rare above that point; a pair of Harporhynchus was seen in the shrub oaks at about 10,000 feet altitude that I thought was *crissalis*, but as they were not taken, the record is open to question.

Campylorhynchus affinis. ST. LUCAS CACTUS WREN. Common as far up the San Telmo Valley as suitable nesting ground was seen, about thirty miles from the coast. Mr. Bryant recorded it from as far north as San Quintin, fifty miles south of San Telmo.

Salpinctes obsoletus. ROCK WREN. One found nesting at 8500 feet; more common on the lower slopes.

Catherpes mexicianus punctulatus. DOTTED CAÑON WREN. Not uncommon in several places on San Pedro.

Thryothorus bewickii spilurus. VIGORS'S WREN. Common along the western slopes of the mountain.

Troglodytes aedon aztecus. WESTERN HOUSE WREN. Abundant in the pines.

Sitta carolinensis aculeata SLENDER-BILLED NUTHATCH. Rather rare but well distributed in the pines.

Sitta pygmæa leuconucha. WHITE-NAPED NUTHATCH. The most abundant species on the mountain; found everywhere in the pines. Upon our arrival May 5 this species was mating; noisy little companies of five or six to a dozen were seen chasing one another through the pines, chattering and calling from daylight till dark; although dozens of nests were discovered all were practically inaccessible. A favorite location for the burrow was on the under side of a dead branch, well away from the trunk of a large pine, and from twenty-five to a hundred feet from the ground. A series of over one hundred and thirty skins sustain the characteristics of the types to a very gratifying degree.

Parus inornatus griseus. GRAY TITMOUSE. Seen in several localities on San Pedro but not at all common. Specimens from the base of the range were identified as *griseus*, but as I have no specimens from the pine belt I can only surmise its identity.

Parus gambeli. MOUNTAIN CHICKADEE. Abundant in the pines but found chiefly in the region of Manzanita and oak thickets. In winter it was seen about Valladares and along the lower valleys.

Chamæa fasciata henshawi. PALLID WREN-TIT. Common along the lower slopes of the mountain and not rare in the highest altitudes where it nests in the shrub oak and Manzanita.

Psaltriparus minimus californicus. CAIFORNIA BUSH-TIT. Not common in the pines, but noted from several localities; very abundant below 3000 feet.

Regulus calendula. RUBY-CROWNED KINGLET. Rather common during migrations.

Turdus ustulatus. RUSSET-BACKED THRUSH. Seen in the pines as late as May 25; a female taken May 21; it is possibly a resident of the pines, but those taken showed little enlargement of the ovaries, and it is more probable that they were belated migrants.

Merula migratoria propinqua. WESTERN ROBIN. Common along the base of the mountain in winter; a few were seen in May, 1889, at La Grulla, but none were noted the past season.

Sialia mexicana. WESTERN BLUEBIRD. Very common during migrations from sea level to the top of the range, a few lingering to nest with the local race. A series of seventy-five skins taken the present year during the nesting season sustain the characters of *anabelæ*, as set forth by myself in 1889, to a strong degree, only about 5% of the males showing an unbroken band of bay on the breast, which refers them to true *mexicana*, and many of the high-plumaged males of the *anabelæ* stripe were almost entirely without bay markings on either breast or scapulæ.

Printed by Libri Plureos GmbH in Hamburg, Germany